Riptionary

Riptionary

✦

Surf Lingo Lexicon

Scott A. Mathews

iUniverse, Inc.

New York Lincoln Shanghai

Riptionary
Surf Lingo Lexicon

iUniverse, Inc.

For information address:
iUniverse, Inc.
2021 Pine Lake Road, Suite 100
Lincoln, NE 68512
www.iuniverse.com

ISBN: 0-595-31100-8

Printed in the United States of America

This book is dedicated to everyone who has ever contributed to the website at Riptionary.com—without you this would not have been possible.

Contents

Acknowledgements

This book is the product of the many surfers around the globe who have taken the time and interest in Riptionary.com to submit their entries. I owe so much to the gesture of goodwill and interest shown in helping Riptionary.com become the internet's most comprehensive online surf lingo content website. I hope this effort is reflective of your generosity and in keeping with the spirit of the sport and venue we hold so dear.

Many thanks go to Nib for your friendship, support and contributions. In the early days of the website, your input was instrumental in steering it in a positive creative direction. There's no doubt without your input, constructive criticism and encouragement it wouldn't be where it is today. You don't often find people of your caliber in life and I feel truly blessed and lucky to consider you as one of my crew.

To my editor, significant other, best friend and surf companion, Jennifer. Thank you for brightening my life with your continual smile and easy-going nature...and for making this into a fun and rewarding project.

To Denise I extend a most sincere, heartfelt, and enduring thanks for our son. Describing what Ethan means to me is almost impossible. You will always hold a special place in my heart.

Lastly I thank Ethan. I am so proud to have you as my son. In the last six years I have learned more about what it means to be a father, friend, and a better person simply by watching you grow up. I love you more than words could ever express.

Introduction

Being an all around waterman and surfer for most of my 39 years, I have grown to love and appreciate surfing and its lifestyle and culture. I created Riptionary.com as a means of uniting surfers and surf lovers of the world through, quite literally, our common language. This book is an extension of that effort. What better way to give back to something that has given me so much?

The Riptionary is distinctive in that it has been compiled from the words of surfers from around the globe. This approach affords visitors, surfers and non-surfers alike, the unique and rare opportunity to take a heuristic journey through the sub-culture that is and defines surfing from a worldwide perspective. As individuals, we're all different, but we are united through our common love of the ocean and the language associated with it. In no other sport does this occur as universally as in surfing.

In the first year alone of Riptionary.com, surfers from around the globe added hundreds of new and interesting terms, phrases and descriptions—and I'm stoked to get more every day. Riptionary.com is growing…almost faster than I can keep up with it.

Surfing is also growing in popularity—and there's no reason to believe this won't continue. While some surfers see this as a problem that translates to crowds at their local break, I see it as an opportunity to spread awareness for the sport and venue we hold so dear. The more people that learn about surfing and its sub-culture, the better off we will all be.

If, through our common language, I can offer just a glimpse into the surfing sub-culture, then perhaps more people will understand why surfing and the ocean mean so much to us and enlist in the cause to protect it. I see that as the ultimate win-win.

I hope you have as much fun reading it as I did putting it together.

A

a-frame. description used by surfers to describe a large wave that forms into a surfable peak rather than a straight line.

accelerate. to gain speed by applying downward force on the surfboard while turning at the bottom portion of wave so that you can climb the face of the wave and setup for a maneuver.

accessory man. derogatory term used by surfers to describe a person who has every piece of the most popular surf gear imaginable, but has no real talent for surfing and only manages to pull off the look.

ace. to be alone or in a solitary state of mind.

acetone. cleaning solvent used in surfboard manufacturing. This is really nasty stuff…highly flammable; toxic.

ache. an endearing term used by surfers to describe how they feel after being rag-dolled or worked by a big ol' gnarly, macking bomb.

acid drop. act of executing a really late take off as a wave is already breaking or about to break; signified by suddenly having the bottom fall out as you free fall down the face of the wave.

action. term used to modify or describe another surfing term. For example, "Check out the action of the boil on the inside."

aerial. part of a maneuver where the surfer and his/her board leaves the water; requires split second timing and is only performed by expert surfers.

ag. a multi-purpose word, pronounced like the ach in German. "ag, no man" (sign of irritation). can precede any sentence for various effects, such as the more neutral, "ag, I do not know." used by some as a stand-alone expletive.

aggro. angry; aggressive or literally out of control. "That dude went "aggro" on that kook when he dropped in on him."

ahoy. a general South African greeting. same as aweh, howzit, yooit, hoesit, yo.

ahua. Hawaiian word used to describe a place close to shore where a broken wave rises, reforms and breaks again; also known as kipapa or puao.

aikona. no way, absolutely not going to happen.

air. act executed by a surfer who, after having gained sufficient speed, rides up the face of a wave and launches off the wave face or lip into the sky.

airbrush. precise tool used by surfboard designers to spray color or graphics onto a surfboard. The tool is powered by an air compressor and sprays paint from a small cylindrical container similar to an aerosol spray can.

aita (aaa-tay). a general South African greeting. "aita brah!"

alaia. an old school Hawaiian term used to describe a surfboard made of wood; generally about six feet long and used by Hawaiians to surf prior to the overthrow of the Hawaiian monarchy in the late 19th century.

alchemy hour. period of time when a surfer enjoys the best a swell has to offer, resulting in a seemingly magical time that has transmuted the surfer and touched his/her soul.

aloha. acknowledgement coined by the Hawaiians; used to signify hello or good-bye; "aloha" has become a universal standard of surfers the world over.

amped. condition whereby a surfer is charged up, stoked, fired-up or psyched; condition generally seen after a particularly exhilarating ride or session.

ancillary stoke. the condition bestowed upon an onlooker or crowd as a surfer pulls off a radical or insane maneuver.

angular spreading. as waves in a train leaves a fetch, they may leave at an angle to the main direction of the wind in the fetch. Thus, swell waves may arrive at a forecast point though it may lie to one side or the other of the main wind line direction.

artificial reef. definition or description used to describe an underwater man-made structure or object that usually causes waves to break where they otherwise would not.

ass munch. derogatory term used by surfers to describe or address a kook, wanna-be, or non-talented surfer who tends to be aggressive and cut off other surfers off on a regular basis; "That ass munch just cut me off!"

ate it. a phrase used by surfers to describe the result of another surfer or one's own unfortunately bad result of a ride; "I ate it so hard on that last bomb when it closed out on me."

atmospheric pressure. the pressure exerted on the Earth's surface caused by the weight of the air in the atmosphere; usually varies from between 950–1050 milli-bars at sea level.

atoll. an island or island chain that consists of a partly submerged coral reef belt surrounding a central lagoon or depression; lagoon island.

arvie. the Australian equivalent of "arvo" or afternoon.

aweh (ah-way). a general South African greeting. "aweh my bru" (hello my friend) Also howzit, yooit, hoesit, yo.

axed. to be crushed, whacked or worked by a wave. "the lip of that gnarly bomb really axed me". also see carrots, drilled.

B

B1F. abbreviation referring to a surfer being thrown from a wave by a sudden change in the wave's shape, particularly the breaking lip.

backdoor. act of pulling into a tube from behind a wave's breaking peak; also the name for a surf spot at Pipeline, Hawaii.

backoff. the term used by surfers to describe a steep wave that has moved from shallow water into a section of deeper water close to shore.; when the wave slope becomes less steep and usually unrideable; often occurs after a wave passes a shallow object such as reef, sandbar, or rock.

backside. term used to describe the act of surfing down the line with your back facing the wave face; Can apply to either regular or goofy footers, depending on the direction down the line the surfer takes.

backwash. description of reflected energy from a wave as it moves back out to sea after having gone up onto the beach or rebounded off an immovable object such as a pier, jetty or other large object.

baggies. surf trunks about knee-length or a little longer; loose fitting shorts that were originally made popular in the 80's but have enjoyed tremendous staying power and popularity due to their practical use in the sport of surfing.

bail. to abandon, jump off or ditch one's board without regard to other surfers in the water; this act is generally executed by those who are not capable of duck diving or turning turtle.

bake. a wave that closes out and dumps without peeling left or right; usually found at beach breaks where predominant wave direction approaches at an almost 90° angle to the shoreline.

bakkie. the term for a pickup truck in South Africa. "ute" in Australia.

balsa. a super-light, porous wood used through the 1940's and 50s as the standard material for surfboard manufacturing; became popular when laminating techniques allowed surfboard cores to be sealed and protected from contact with water.

bamboo. natural substance that can be used as a replacement for fiberglass in the surfboard manufacturing process, but is not used much today.

banana hammock. derogatory term used by surfers to describe the swimsuits worn by muscle beach kooks and non-surfers; wearing a banana Hammock while surfing is not only considered taboo, but is just plain weird; commonly known in the Northeast as "banana benders."

bangbroek. South African term for being wigged-out or generally scared over surf conditions.

bannocked. to get an open cut from any surfing activity.

bark the dog. the South African translation for the act of barfing. same as kotch, park a tiger, blow chunks or show a Technicolor yawn.

barney. derogatory term used to describe someone who is less than skilled at surfing; originally derived from a popular cartoon character because his geekness seems to be in parallel with the acts and general demeanor of a hodad.

barn waller. derogatory term used to describe someone who is seen as a kook, barney, or just plain old stink-bugging surfer with a poor style; "That guy is barn walling down the line".

barnyard. another name for a kook, beginner, wave hog, non-surfer coming out and screaming about how they're ripping when they're actually stink bugging, squatting, and surfing with the poorest style possible; also a commonly applied moniker to high school jocks, preppies, and others who are trying to fit into the surf community.

barrel. a hollow, pitching wave that allows you to tuck inside.

bashing. body surfing; term also used to describe what a surfer does when he smacks the lip.

bathymetry. term used to describe the bottom contour of a break. Actually means the measurement of depth of bodies of water.

beachbreak. waves breaking over a sandy bottom, generally close to the shore.

beachcomber. originally coined as defining a destitute or degraded individual who frequents a beach front, but more recently sanitized as being anyone enamored of spending time in or around the ocean; reference to a long sweeping wave.

beat down. term used to describe someone who has been worked or rag-dolled by a wave or had their butt kicked on the beach for snaking someone once too often.

beavertail. the moniker associated with a 70's wetsuit design featuring a large flap that was wrapped under the crotch and secured in the front.

beef. a problem or situation where someone is angry with another person; the issue at hand that causes turmoil.

bennie. term used by New Jersey locals to describe New York tourists that invade the beaches during the summer months; bennies wear tanks while in the ocean and sandals with socks.

benny. someone who dresses like, talks like, acts like, and hangs out with actual hardcore surfers, but is not one; he or she may know how to surf but do not do it on a regular basis and are generally not very good; a benny is somewhat of a "surfer-poser", but still a generally cool label to have.

bent. an old school body surfing term used to describe what one feels like after having executed a poorly and often painful conclusion to a ride.

bergwind. the hot, dry wind that blows offshore on the west coast. typically blows from the northeast. on the east coast it blows from the north or northwest. "check out groundswell textured into glassy perfection by the light bergwind."

betty. term used by surfers to describe a good looking wahine or group of wahines; according to some sources this was originally derived from a popular cartoon character.

biltong. the South African equivalent to what we call "jerky (US)."

biscuit. the South African term for a cookie or an insult aimed at a twit or a fool.

bitchin'. term used by surfers in the 50s and 60s to signify that something was cool, top-notch, and excellent.

blank. foam block used as the starting point of a surfboard.

blasted. term used to describe what happens when a wave unloads and works, rag dolls, or otherwise drills a surfer.

bleak. to be disappointed or sad. "bru, I was so bleak after that flat spell.

blow chunks. to vomit, bark the dog, park the tiger, Technicolor yawn.

blown Out. description of ocean conditions when the wind blows so hard that the surf is chopped up and rendered unrideable.

boatman. guide who takes you via boat to remote locations to surf non-crowded spots; generally, the term is used for surfari type trips, but can be used for local spots that are only accessible by boat.

bodyboard. boards made of sponge and ridden on one's stomach. A Boogie™ Board is a paipoboard modified in 1971 by Tom Morey to ride dangerous shallow reefs safely; body boarders often augment their ride with swim-fins.

boggas. a derivative term of affection used by surfers to describe a totally outrageous wave that either has a big tube or nice shaped shoulder.

bogus. term used by surfers to describe someone or something that is just plain wrong or really, really lame.

bomb. a large, hard-breaking wave that closes out usually by rising, pitching, and dumping over.

bombora. Australian term for big waves that break farther away from shore; also called bombie or cloudbreak.

bonzer. Australian term that is equivalent slang for bitchin'; the Campbell brothers of Southern California adopted the term in the 70's for their five-fin surfboard.

boost. to get airborne as in "boost off the lip."

bottom. refers to the ocean floor or to the lowest part of the wave the surfer can ride on—the bottom of the wave.

bottom contour. the shape of the bottom of a surfboard from rail-to-rail; e.g. concave or vee.

bottom turn. A sweeping move that enables the surfer to establish speed and direction for a ride; establishes the rhythm of the ride as the surfer gets in synch the wave; by far the most crucial turn in surfing as it sets the tempo for the entire ride.

bowl. a section of a given wave in which the line of the wave raps toward the shore as the wave begins to drag on bottom contour objects (sandbar, reef or rocks); effect often causes the wave to gain speed, form into a peak, or grow more hollow or steep.

bowled. another way of saying tubed, green room, shacked, etc; "Did you see me get bowled on that last left?"

brah. surf brother, associate, peer, colleague, friend in liquid solidarity; anyone on this planet, including women who shares the love of surfing; derived from bruddah, Hawaiian pidgin for brother.

brahbonics. a term used to describe surf lingo and its colorful vernacular.

brain freeze. the feeling in the cranium and sinus cavity immediately after the first duck-dive when paddling out in very cold water; characterized by an instant and often, excruciating ice cream headache.

brand-x. reference to anything of inferior composition, execution or condition; "Man that was strictly Brand-X;" television colloquialism adopted pre short board era.

brasse (brah-ser). South African equivalent to "crew", or a group of friends.

breaking. when a wave moves from deep water into a shallow area the wave's energy is projected vertically as it rebounds; also called "shoaling;" as the wave energy is projected the face becomes unstable and the lip of the wave tumbles or "breaks" down the face of the wave.

break line. the point in the lineup where waves begin to break; as a general rule, waves tend to begin breaking when they reach water depths of approximately 1.3 times the wave face height.

breakup. an occurrence whereby waves approach a beach and split into different peaks or lines with a clear separation between rideable shoulders; usually caused by the convergence of two swells from different directions and or periods overlapping the same break; also called "scattered peaks."

brah. buddy or friend; also used in greetings as in "Howzit Brah?"

brodad. surfer or hodad wanna-be surfer who overuses the terms bro or brah.

bru. the South African term used for a friend, bruddah, brah, etc.

bruddah. common term used by surfers when describing fellow surfers; also used as a greeting, and is synonymous with bro; not gender specific, also used to greet wahines.

bucket. helmet usually used for surfing over shallow reef or rocks.

buffalo-eye. similar to the stink-eye, but longer in duration; conveys gravity or seriousness.

bummed. disappointed, mad about things not going your way.

bump. euphemism for a swell; often used to describe what's coming on the horizon.

bumps. build-up of wax on a surfboard deck added to cause friction to hold the rider's footing during a ride.

bumpy. choppy water or wave face; could be a decent wave, but some bumps on the face may make it difficult to ride.

buoy. a surfer's best tool, telling such things as wind, swell direction, period duration, barometric pressure, and temperature; tells everything we need to know in order to justify getting up at 0'dark-thirty in the morning; thanks NOAA!

burleigh heads. right point which was made famous by the Stubbies surf contents being held there.

burn. to take off past a grommet or someone on a wave; similar to snake, but without a drop-in or slash cutback in front.

busted. to be caught in the act of something devious or subversive.

butt breach. occurrence when you first surface after having been worked by a bomb that caused you to lose your bathing suit bottom/board shorts.

C

C5. five fin design with three main fins and two canards; very stable setup that reduces turbulence over the main three fins relieving pressure and drag on outboard fins, in turn creating more drive.

cactus juiced. to experience a type of injury that leaves you unable to surf.

canards. smaller and outermost fins of the C5 fin system; designed to reduce turbulence to the surfboard's main three fins.

cant. angling of the outside fins toward the rail so that the inner angle is 90 degrees + some number; makes the board handle better on its rails

cape doctor. the southeastern wind that often howls at gale-force strength in the summer time.

capillary wave. small waves where wind is often the disturbing force and surface tension of the water is the restoring force.

carbon fiber. a strong, light and durable fiber that, when soaked in resin, creates an extremely strong, lightweight material; sometimes placed in strips along the length of a board during glassing to help prevent creasing.

carrots. to be or get rag dolled, broken, done over, thrashed, worked.

carve. semi-symmetrical, fluid turn; also used to describe the abilities of a surfer; "Dude, the Bruddah can carve."

cashed. derived from smoking-related happenings, once the flame goes out; used in place of being tired, relaxed, done.

caught inside. when a surfer is trapped between the shoreline and breaking waves; generally causes a surfer to wait for a lull between sets for a chance to paddle back out.

central pressure index (CPI). minimum atmospheric pressure in the eye or center of a hurricane; used to estimate the wind velocities in the storm; the lower the CPI, the greater the wind's velocity.

channel. a relatively deep spot where the waves do not normally break; often where receding water flows back out to sea.

charf. to tease someone, joke around, make fun of, or flirt with the opposite sex in an attempt to ("spadework")…you get the idea.

charger. someone who pushes themselves with all they have; "He charged that overhead wave!"

chariot. a car. "That bra has a styling chariot."

cheater five. five toes to the nose; keeping your weight back on the board to maintain trim and speed, squat down and extend one foot forward and hang five toes over the nose of your surfboard; a longboard maneuver.

chill. to calm down when not getting good waves.

chips. an expletive issued when you're about to get worked by that bomb closing out on your head.

chop. very small waves on the surface created by local winds.

chuck. to leave, depart, go, split, flee, etc.

church of the open sky. affectionate term surfers use to describe the ocean and what one experiences when they partake in her offerings.

claim. the proclamation exhibited by waving ones arms in the air. Especially after an exceptionally good ride or maneuver.

classic. something that is epic, excellent, perfect, incredible, etc.

claw hands. when your hands are too cold to open or close anything; condition brought on from surfing in frigid water.

clean. faces are not rippled or blown by wind; usually occurs when wind is off-shore or blowing lightly.

cleanup set. a group of rogue waves that break on the outside, generally working everyone in the lineup.

cleanup wave. a single wave that breaks outside of the lineup, dumping on everyone; also called a rogue.

clidro. the process when a surfer turns up and down the face of a wave while surfing down the line; used to describe the technique for gaining speed as a surfer traverses the wave face.

clipped. The occurrence when the breaking lip of a wave knocks a surfer off of their board.

close out. when waves break across a bay or normally safe channel rendering a surf spot unrideable because surfers cannot paddle out to the line-up; also used to describe waves that dump, leaving no rideable wave face.

cloud nine. term used for a floater; to traverse across the lip of a breaking wave as it closes out.

clucked. afraid; intimidated; all around scared by a wave.

cnoid waves. as waves come in to shallow water their shape changes to something called a cnoid which has a short, steep crest and long shallow trough; these are what we see as waves approaching from the horizon.

coffee brick. the heavy feeling in one's stomach after drinking too much coffee before a session.

cold front. the leading edge of an advancing cold air mass that is under running and displacing the warmer air in its path; generally, with the passage of a cold front, the temperature and humidity decrease, the pressure rises, and the wind shifts (usually from the southwest to the northwest in the Northern Hemisphere); precipitation is generally at, or behind the front, and with a fast-moving system, a squall line may develop ahead of the front.

combo-swell. a combination of swells from varying directions creating peaky and crossed up sections as waves converge; combo swells are great for most beach breaks but break up the perfect lines at most reef and point breaks.

computer aided design/manufacture (CAD/CAM). software tool used by some shapers to cut blanks known as "pre-shapes;" the process reduces man-hours of shaping allowing manufacturers to offer significantly less expensive boards to consumers; surfers often perceive these boards as inferior in quality, but when viewed with a laser gauge, they have been proven to be much more accurate than hand shaping.

concave. soft chine indentation running lengthways on the bottom of a board, designed to create lift and reduce drag on the surfboard hull.

consistent. condition of the sea when waves are coming in at regular intervals and breaking in a predictable manner.

continental shelf. underwater portion of a land mass that extends from a continent out to sea to a depth of approximately one-thousand feet.

contour. nautical map/chart indicator representing points of equal value compared to datum or starting point.

cook. a terms used to describe good surf. when the surf is cooking, it is "going off", "firing", "pumping", "cranking", "cracking", etc. if someone "cooks", they're either a really good surfer or having a killer session.

corduroy. used to describe the appearance of a swell or a set of waves approaching the lineup from the horizon.

core. a surfer who goes out in all conditions no matter what the air/sea temp is or how good the waves are.

corn skin. the outer glass layer of a surfboard that has yellowed from delamination, or exposure to too much sun or water.

corner. shoulder or end section of a breaking wave; often used to describe closeouts that exhibit an area where the water stays relatively turbulence free.

covered. tubed; pitted; shacked.

cowabunga. term said to exude happiness or to describe the act of being overjoyed.

crazy. catching a wave so large and gnarly that to some it seems way beyond comprehension why anyone would ever do it; surfers are often categorized as crazy to non-surfers.

crease. damage usually exhibited by a fracture line running across the board on bottom, deck or both; often occurs when a fellow surfer's fins ride across another board during a ride.

crest. top portion of a wave or the effect occurring as a wave begins to break.

crew. group that surfs together, usually at the same break or area.

crib. another terms used to describe ones abode. Same as house, apartment, shack. Any place someone crash's can be "crib."

critical section. hardest and most challenging portion of the wave.

crook. something or someone that is no good is said to be "crooked."

cross-chop. condition occurring when side-shore wind (parallel to shoreline) is strong enough to cause the peaks of waves to be blown out of a line; not good for a go-out.

crumbeater. a person who is the lowest in the pecking order; a grovler, wanna be grom waiting for scraps. subject to ridicule and torture. crumbeaters that are extremely persistent may move into higher orders over time…maybe. for example; "Give that one to the crumbeater."

curl. the curl of the wave; the inner pitching or folding part of the wave.

current. parallel flow of water along a coastal area beach.

cut out. term used to describe the exiting of a wave; pull-out or kick-out.

cutback. a 180-degree turn that is done on either of the two rails of the surfboard; to turn back toward the curl or breaking part of a wave.

cyclone. an air mass that rotates counter-clockwise in the Northern Hemisphere and clockwise in the Southern Hemisphere; can consist of high-pressure or low-pressure.

D

da bomb. the absolute best of something; can be used to describe a person, place or thing…pretty much anything.

da kine. Hawaiian-style talk for the best kind of wave.

dawn patrol. getting up before sunrise in order to catch the best waves with the least amount of crowding; this time of day usually offers the cleanest conditions before the wind picks up.

dead presidents. description of US Currency, alluding to portraiture displayed on the notes; example, "I can't get a new wetsuit 'til I harvest some more dead presidents;" also known as wampum, dinero, jing, scratch, dough, gelt, cash.

deck/grip pad. rough-surfaced material (neoprene or other substance) that is adhered to the deck of a surfboard to increase traction; used in lieu of wax; most often used on the surfboard tail for added traction for the trailing foot.

deep water breaks. surf spots where swells have a drastic transition from deep water (1000 feet or more) to a more shallow area; these include offshore breaks like the Cortez Banks where long period (16 sec. +) swell hits the reef and rapidly projects vertically.

degrees. navigational term used to measure latitude and longitude; with minutes and seconds used as fractional measurements between degrees.

delaminate. when the bond between the fiberglass and foam of a surfboard breaks down and separates; usually caused by water breaching the fiberglass; can also occur when a surfboard is over exposed to direct sunlight or heat.

derelict. Cool; sick; dope; used to describe something really cool.

diffraction. when waves encounter a surface-piercing obstacle, such as a breakwater or an island.

ding. indentation or crack in the outer surface of a surfboard; damage to the surfboard that causes the integrity of the glassed surface to crack or delaminate from the foam core; minor or "pressure" dings (not requiring repair) are caused by riding choppy or bumpy waves and are illustrated by small circular spots on the board's surface.

direction. defines where the waves, wind or swell is coming from; note: direction always identifies where the swell or the wind is "coming from," not the direction it is "moving/blowing to".

diva. another name for a wahine or female surfer, especially one that rips.

dodgy. something or someone that is of a suspicious nature.

dogging. going backside in the pit, green room, shack, front porch, etc.

don the apron. to eat with malicious fervor…like one has not had a meal in some time. usually occurs after a exceptionally long and taxing session. "dude! I'm so hungry; I'm going to need to don the apron when I get home."

double overhead. unit of measure that surfers use to describe a wave that is two times as tall as its rider.

double up. when one wave overtakes or combines with another; creates very powerful waves.

down rail. where the deck curves down to meet the flat bottom at a hard edge.

down the line. a reference to a point further along the crest of a wave from the location from where a surfer drops in.

drag. the coefficient of friction that causes water to be slowed as flows along surfboard surfaces; most pronounced in the leading edges of a surfboard: the forward rail line, the forward rocker and outline, and the leading edges of fins.

drilled. to get worked, axed, dumped, smoked, rag dolled.

drive. the effect of water pressure being exerted against the bottom surface of a surfboard.

drop. the initial downward slide on the face of wave after taking off and before the bottom turn.

drop in. used to describe catching a wave that is already occupied; taking off on the shoulder while someone is taking off deeper…not a good thing.

drop in late. catching the steepest part of a wave at the wave's most critical time; often results in an acid drop or wipeout.

dropped wallet. a term invented by Tom Curren in reference to the act of lying back on the wave face to maintain control of ones board.

duck dive. technique where a surfer will dive under/through a breaking wave at its base to avoid getting worked.

ducked. leave, book, jet flee, depart "As soon as it went flat we ducked."

dude. term used for surfing buddies or as a general reference to a male surfer.

dudette. Female surfing buddy.

dumping. used to describe waves or the sea state that causes waves to close out with little to no chance of getting a decent ride.

dune. a big, peaking wave; usually a longer period swell that builds energy as it approaches the shallow area and jacks up.

duration. the length of time the wind blows during a swell generation event; also one of the central tenets in wave generation along with fetch and velocity.

E

eddy. the circular movement of water usually formed where currents pass obstructions, between two adjacent currents flowing counter to each other, or along the edge of a permanent current.

egg beater. a person who sits in the lineup frantically paddling for waves yet catches none; derived from the chaotic motion of their arm movement.

egg. refers to the dull rounded shape of a surfboard nose, tail or rail.

el naio. occurs when warm equatorial waters move in and displace the colder waters of the Humboldt Current, cutting off the upwelling process.

el nino. a weak, warm current appearing annually around Christmas time along the coast of Ecuador and Peru and lasting only a few weeks to a month or more; observed when the easterly trade winds weaken, allowing warmer waters of the western Pacific to migrate eastward and eventually reach the South American Coast.

el rollo. originally an old school term used by BB in The Endless Summer to describe a CC move; currently most applicable to bodyboarders; props to Bruce Brown.

energy. the unit of measure for determining the power of a wave; usually in meters or centimeters squared.

entry. term used to describe the area of the surfboard where water first comes into contact with the rocker.

epic. beyond the usual or ordinary; generally used in the positive sense, as in, "The conditions were epic today."

epoxy. plastic resin used by some manufacturers in lieu of polyester resin; user usually also uses a polystyrene blank.

equatorial trough. the quasi-continuous area of low pressure between the sub-tropical high pressure centers in both the Northern and Southern Hemisphere.

exposure. term used to describe how breaks within an area will receive an incoming swell relative to the direction it faces as the incoming swell arrives.

expression session. phrase used to describe when contest organizers offer surfers an opportunity to just go out and surf however they want.

extra tropical. term used to indicate that a hurricane or typhoon has lost its "tropical" characteristics and has begun to weaken.

eye wall. a deep, thick band of clouds that surround the eye or center of hurricanes and typhoons; typically where the strongest winds of a storm are found.

eye. a relatively calm area found near the center of hurricanes and typhoons.

F

FCS. Fin Control System. Five fin setup; three main and two canards (C5 Models).

face height. height measurement taken from the front of the wave; measured from the top of the crest to the low part of the trough.

face. the front part of the wave; surfers ride primarily on the wave face.

fade. to carve in the opposite direction of a take off point regardless of wave shape.

fading. the act of dropping into a wave and turning away from the steepest part of the face. usually done as a positioning maneuver in lieu of fading to get back into the pocket.

fakey. a bottom turn or carve back toward the whitewater or curl of the wave; "He went fakey."

fall line. an anal description of the best and fastest place to drop in; usually just to the edge of the folding lip or the highest point on the wave as it begins to break.

falls. term used to describe the appearance of the pitching lip of the wave; top portion of a wave generated as it throws toward shore.; not a good spot.

fan. a wall of spray off a carving turn; usually executed at the top of the wave face or lip; makes a nice show for the crew.

fascist. originally, a member of the Fascist, formed by Benito Mussolini, a political movement espousing extremely anti-democratic principles; in the surfer's world, individuals with no regard or respect for their fellow surfers are fascist.

feather. term used to describe the occurrence of mist blowing off the lip of a breaking wave by offshore winds.

fetch. the distance over which wind blows in a swell generation event; also one of the central tenets in wave generation along with wind duration and velocity.

fiberglass. finely spun glass strands woven together to provide a cloth sheeting used in surfboard lamination. Adds strength and durability to the foam core or surfboard "blank".

fin box. the piece that is cut into the foam blank and glassed in to hold board fins; e.g. FCS, futures, red-x, etc.

fins. devices used for directional control while surfing.

fin throw. a semi-radical maneuver executed by a surfer in which the boards fins are broken loose from the wave. the result is generally a huge spray from the board as this move takes a sharp aggressive change in direction that displaces a significant amount of water.

fin waft. similar to a fin throw, but the fins only briefly appear above the wave before a surfer brings the board back down the face. also known as simply....waft.

firin'. term used to describe really good surf; pumping, macking or goin' off.

first peak. the rebound off of the jetty that forms a perfect bowling wave; at Sebastian Inlet the peak is called "first peak" as it is in other parts of the US where there are jetties and piers.

fish. term used to describe a shortboard with added width and thickness, designed to improve wave catching capability while maintaining performance; used in small or mushy conditions.

flailer. another name for kook, poor styled surfer, stinkbug, or barney.

flair. another term used to describe someone that is surfing exceptionally well. conditions "go off" surfers "flair".

flat. when there are no waves to surf it is said to be "flat."

flick-off. maneuver used to kick the board clear of the breaking wave; step-off.

flick. an increase in the rate of rocker near the nose.

flip. a 360 air in which a surfer performs a complete flip and lands on the back of the wave as it breaks.

flip-flop. the unofficially sanctioned footwear of surfers; one of the unspoken standards.

floater. where the surfer rides his board loosely along the top of the breaking up or foam of the wave.

fluff. spray dispersing off the lip of a breaking wave.

foam. the description of the whitewater that forms as a result of a wave having broken.

fo-flat. wave conditions that exist during a flat spell; implies more than just that it is flat, but that it has been flat and may remain flat for extended periods of time; coined by Don the klank Klankhauf circa 1969 during a Sunday afternoon cocktail party during a flat spell in which he complained; "It's so flat it is fo-flat!."

foam. the liquid polyethylene material used to mold surfboard blanks; hardens into a firm material that is shaped into the final product; also used to describe the whitewater of a breaking wave.

foamer. a person who rides the foam whitewater of the wave.

foil. the distribution of thickness from the nose to tail of a surfboard.

four one one, need 411. adopted from the former Bell System information number; applied today in a broader sense, i.e.; "Did you get the 411 on the weather today?"

Franklins. specific application of dead presidents, describing US currency; a one-hundred dollar bill displays the portrait of Benjamin Franklin; "That's a nice board, but it'll run you six Franklins."

free boarding. generally refers to the act of riding a surfboard behind a boat, similar to water skiing; skurfing.

freight train. descriptive term applied to a very strong and very fast wave.

freight train barrel. term used to describe a really fast moving wave that suddenly jacks and pitches as it forms a nice hollow barrel.

frequency downshifting. increase in wave period within a fetch; a decrease in frequency is an increase in period.

friggin'. what one says when he/she gets snaked; as in "You friggin' kook!."

front porchin' it. a way of describing the action of a surfer who is cruising down the line in the waves vortex just under the pitching lip.

frontside. to surf down the line facing the wave.

frost. fine, hot, sexy, cute; "Check him out—he is frosted!;" "He is always frostin' at me." (looking good for my enjoyment).

frosted. the term used to describe when a surfer sprays someone paddling back out to the lineup; spackled.

fudge tunnel. description of a tube at a break where the water is yellow or brown; can be anywhere in the world where there is water pollution.

Fujiwara effect. when two tropical storms rotate around each other; caused by the lack of steering winds in the upper atmosphere.

full-on. going for it; all out; having a really killer session.

full suit. a wetsuit that covers the entire body; also known as a "steamer" in Australia, Ireland and some other parts of the world.

funboard. term used to describe a mid-size board designed for ease of ride in small conditions; a mid-sized board that usually has the shape of an egg, pickle, or a longboard nose; generally ridden by beginners, individuals who start surfing at 30+ years old, and reformed bodyboarders (spongers); very easy to catch waves on and an all around fun board to ride.

G

g'day. traditional Australian salutation, used by surfers and non-surfers alike.

gale warning. an advisory issued for a weather event when sustained surface winds are reported or forecasted to be in the range of 34 to 47 knots over the water.

gash. very sharp turn; gnarly reef cut.

geek. term used by surfers to describe someone who is able to surf, but just barely; lacking in style, grace and the ability to maintain the calm, cool and collected demeanor often displayed by accomplished surfers.

geeked. term used to describe a surfer as he enthusiastically relates the last good go-out to the members of the crew who missed it; usually involves hand surfing and an inability to maintain the usual calm, cool demeanor.

gelcoat. a final coat of thin, hard resin applied to surfboards in order to bring up a slick, shiny uniform surface for finishing.

Gidget. originally coined to indicate a female surfer of diminutive stature; syllabic combination of girl and midget; nickname of a woman named Kathy Kohner whose father wrote a book about her in 1957.

glass-off. figure of speech used by surfers to describe water when the surface is as smooth as glass.

glasser. a moniker for a person who laminates surfboards.

glassy. condition of calm on the ocean; used to describe the optimum conditions to surf in; occurs when there is just a clean breaking swell with no wind on it.

glide. a spiritual place when everything seems to be in synch; the wave, the surfer and the board are one entity; when a surfer achieves this he is said to have "the glide."

glory trail. the same act as prone out, but this is usually accompanied by whoops and hollers from the waiting crowd that just witnessed a surfer ride a wave exceptionally well that caused ancillary stoke to occur.

GMT. Greenwich Mean Time; the Greenwich Meridian is located at 0 degrees longitude, over a town named Greenwich, England. GMT is World Time and the basis of every time zone on the planet; fixed all year and does not switch to daylight savings time. All other time zones have a GMT correction to determine local time. For Standard time, New York is minus 5 hours from GMT, and California is minus 8 hours. So if GMT was 1200, California would be 0400 Pacific Standard Time. GMT is also sometimes called Zulu Time, especially on weather charts which may display 12Z for 1200 GMT (Noon), or 00Z for 0000 GMT (Midnight).

gnarly. depicting an unrideable or intimidating wave; something really bad.

go off. term used to describe a surf spot breaking under optimum conditions; as in, Dude! It's going off!"

go-abb. another name surfers use to label a geek.

go-out. a surf session. used for various meanings related to time spent in the h2o.

goin' off. term used to describe a break under optimum conditions; a perfect breaking wave is said to be goin' off; anything that is beyond good.

golden fold. description of a breaking wave's curl just before sunset when the waning sun casts a golden hue on the face of the wave.

goofy foot. rider who surfs with the right foot as the lead foot.

goons. locals that rule their turf with an iron hand on land and in the lineup.

gouge. sharp and fast turn; damage to a surfboard from reef, rock, etc.

green room. the vortex or location on the wave face where the surfer is covered by the pitching lip.

gremmie, grem. pre-shortboard era reference to a youthful or beginner surfing enthusiast; derivation of gremlin; impish gnomes blamed by airmen of WWII for interfering with mechanical devices; modern term is grommet or grom.

grom board. an extremely short, shortboard. owned by a grommet with extreme surfing capabilities. The board is usually around four and a half to five foot in length.

grommet, grom. modern term for a young surfer; not generally used as a slam unless in conjunction with and expletive.

ground swell. well-shaped waves formed over a great distance; very powerful; usually have more than 11 seconds in a period between wave crests.

gun. a surfboard that is long, narrow, and pointy (both at the nose and the tail) for maximum rail contact; for riding big waves; usually thick and heavy and ranging in length from 7' to 10'; elephant gun; rhino chaser.

gunned. refers to the size of your board in relation to wave conditions; if you don't have the right size board you may be under gunned or over gunned.

gutter. another description of a channel that forms in between or on the side of the break.

H

hack. a drastic and sudden change of direction executed by a surfer. similar to a hard, slashing carving cutback.

hairy. occurrence where a surfer finds himself engaged in a situation that could turn gnarly at any second; think of the drop in at Pipe, that's hairy.

hammered. when a big wave breaks right on top of you, you get hammered.

hang loose. being in a relaxed metabolic and clear-minded state; inverse application of uptight, circa 60s.

hang ten. all ten toes on the nose; gotta be on a log to do this one.

hangin'. an occurrence whereby one just stays put; generally conveys a genuine state of content.

haole. term used to describe surfers in Hawaii who are non-native; derogatory reference to a non-local; derivation of Howlee.

hard rail. sharp, thin-edged surfboard; primarily on performance short boards.

harpooning. to cop wood while surfing.

head dip. longboard trick whereby the rider briefly dips his head into the wave face while riding.

hectic. used to describe something that is radical, extreme, etc. the video was…hectic, bra!

heenalu. Hawaiian term for riding a surfboard; surfing; translates as "wave sliding."

herky jerky. the motion or body movement exhibited by a less than fluid surfer.

high pressure. an area of relative pressure maximum that has diverging winds and a rotation opposite to the earth is rotation; fair weather is typically associated with high pressure.

hindcast. the act of using past weather information to forecast the wave characteristics for a concluded weather event; as in "You should have been here yesterday."

hit the lip. a maneuver in which a surfer turns the surfboard up to schwack the falling lip of the wave and then turns it back down, allowing the board to be repositioned down the face of the wave.

hoakey. orginally coined "Hocus Pocus;" adopted later as Hokey Pokey; subsequent abbreviation to hokey; trickery, illusionary. something unusual, never before witnessed. applied as a good or bad event or circumstance.

hodad. a beginner or non-surfer; one that has yet to master the art of surfing; most of us are hodad's to some degree.

hodaddy. derogatory term used to describe someone who does not surf or is posing as a surfer to be part of the "in" crew at the beach; a poser; someone that surfers prefer not to associate with and tend to avoid once identified.

hold down. to be worked by a wave so big that it holds you under water for what seems like forever.

hollow. extremely concave curling wave; a good thing.

hollow board. Surfboard type invented by Tom Blake in 1932 using redwood sheets to create a long, narrow board much lighter in weight relative to the solid redwood boards of the time.

honey. a female surfer; old school, but it is still hangin' around; term of affection; a good thing to be called!

hoodie. hooded sweatshirt.

hoot. howling and yelling approval and encouragement to buddies.

horde. a multitude, mob or crowd. interchangable for populace description in or out of the water.

hot curl. surfboard type invented in the 1950s by Dale Velzy of California.

hot dog budget. to head out on a surfari with little to no money.

hot dogger/hot dogging. term originally used in the 50s and 60s as a moniker for the surfer who likes to show-off on a longboard; currently used to describe what surfers do to gain speed in weak surf; characterized by a large amount of leg pumping and back-and-forth tracking on the wave.

hot-shot. an experienced surfer who likes to show off but also often starts trouble; totally rude and competitive; thinks he/she owns the waves.

hot coat. a coat of resin applied during the laminating process after the initial coat of resin and glass; so named because the resin and catalyst are mixed to force a fast gelling (more catalyst = faster cure time); the hot coat seals the glass-resin layer, fills any surface imperfections, and is later finish sanded.

howlee. a kook in and out of the water; another derivation of the Hawaiian word "Haole."

howlie. howlie comes from the movie *North Shore*; someone from the mainland who thinks he can surf, but really can't!

howzit. a greeting exchanged among surfers when one pulls up to check a break and encounters another already assessing the situation; as in "How is it?"

huia. an especially high wave formed by the meeting of two crests; said to characterize the surf of Kaipaloaoa, Hawaii.

hull. a bottom shape similar to a boat hull, in which the bottom density thickens out from the stringer to the rails; most common in longboards designed before the late 60s.

humboldt current. aka the Peruvian Current; flows offshore northward along the western side of the South American countries of Chile and Peru.

hundreds. word meaning good, excellent, enjoyable. "hey bra, that session was the hundreds."

hurricane. tropical storm that develops maximum sustained winds of 74 mph or greater; also referred to as typhoons or cyclones in some parts of the world.

hurricane advisory. a formal advisory issued by forecasters at the National Hurricane Center when they have determined that hurricane conditions are expected in a coastal area or group of islands within a 24-hour period.

hurricane season. the period of time from mid-summer thru early fall when the conditions favor the development of tropical disturbances.

hurricane watch. the formal advisory issued by forecasters at the National Hurricane Center when they have determined that conditions are/will be a potential threat to a coastal area or group of islands within a 24- to 36-hour period.

hybrid. surfboards ranging from 7'–9' that give some of the floatation and paddling ease of a longboard as well as the performance of a shortboard.

hydrodynamics. branch of physics concerned with the application of forces producing motion in fluids; as surfers we are all students and practitioners of this science.

I

impact zone. point where the waves break for the first time; shore-side of a breaking wave.

inside. refers to where you are in the line-up, or a place relative to the break; facing an oncoming wave; also refers to a position relative to the shoreline, as in, "He got worked on the inside."

inside the Pope's living room. to be inside the barrel of a wave.

irie. a state of nirvana for Rastafarians…or surfers. made popular by the late Marley, the g-daddy of the ol' school rasta crew.

isobar. lines of equal atmospheric pressure on a weather chart; the proximity to each other and degree of closeness indicates wind velocity within isobars.

isobath. a line connecting points of equal depth below a datum to measure bathymetry and an isobar when used to depict low and high atmospheric pressure readings.

it's all good. term used to describe all the elements involved in getting optimum waves; wind, tide, swell direction, bathymetry, etc.

J

jack. term used to describe what happens as deep ocean swells approach the more shallow water near land or object (reef, rock, etc.); when wave energy is translated into an upward motion building the wave's height and power.

jacked. to have your car trashed or to get jumped by locals in the parking lot.

jacking. the term used to describe a really good swell. "The surf is jacking, Brah."

jag. to take rest; the break after a long session of getting worked.

jammin'. having a good time; listening to your favorite tunes.

jetty. a channel or river mouth whose entry/exit is bordered on both sides by rock or concrete walls; enables a wave to align itself and break consistently away from it as it travels down the wall.

jones/jonesn'. new wave vernacular spelling; an unfulfilled desire; "I'm jonesn' for a go-out."

joy. Aussie term for stoked; sick joy, joyous.

juice. term used to describe the power of any given wave; mega juice, juiced, and wicked juice are all terms for a really powerful wave; only used when the surf is powerful.

juicy. an awesome wave that leaves you wanting more; also used to describe a hot/sexy surfer.

junkyard dog. a name for a surfer who is used to surfing small junky waves; usually has a poor style.

K

karma. your inner spirit; your Chi, bruddah; makes surfing and riding what the ocean has to offer a life-enhancing experience.

kick. extreme rise in the last six inches of the surfboard's rocker; like "flick" at the other end.

kick out. to exit a wave with exceptional style and grace.

kickin'. Cool, sweet, awesome; as in "That was kickin'."

kished. to be "kished" is to be exhausted or really tired after a go-out/session.

knot. the marine term for judging speed/velocity; equals approximately 1.2 miles per hour on land.

kook. wanna be surfers that think they know what is up, enough said.

kook cord. term used for a leash, leg rope, etc.

kookabarn. generally characterized by a wanna-be surfer who exhibits geeked-out characteristics; can be used to describe someone who exhibits geeked-out behavior after a extraordinary ride; "Dude! Quit being such a kookabarn."

kookabunga. the exaltation a kookabarn makes when charging a wave; usually results in a trip over the falls or a bout of pearlitis

koot-kot. term coined by the late Gregory Lee Smith; another derivative of the word kook; a barney or surfer who thinks they are significantly better than they actually are; "That guy stinkbugging down the line is a koot-kot!"

kootamouskotzy. description of a kook, koot, kookabarn, barnyard, barnwaller, or individual who is of the highest order of kook imaginable.

kootzky. a term used for a kook who is flying down the line quickly and out of control with a stinkbug stance; "That guy is a major kootzky."

kowabunga. expressed initially by Chief Rain Cloud of the Howdy Doody Show, circa late 50s; revived by Bart Simpson, circa late 80s; rallying cry for riders of surf, snow and street.

kulana nalu. the place where a surfer paddles to catch a wave; usually the most distant line of breakers.

L

lacerate. term meaning a sudden, sharp, carving term. can also be used to describe a maneuver performed by a surfer.

la nina. the affect caused by the cooling of the ocean surface off the western coast of South America; the opposite effect of an el nino weather event/pattern.

lagooned. the act of being flushed into a lagoon after being worked by a bomb; generally occurs at a reef break.

lake Atlantic. condition found on the US east coast when the lack of swell causes the ocean to look like a lake; occurs frequently during the summer months.

lala. to surf diagonally on the face of the wave; a wave to the right; with muku, a wave to the left; or, the seaward side of a cresting wave.

laminate. the first coat of resin applied to a shaped surfboard blank; laminating resin is used to soak the fiberglass cloth and adhere it to the blank; the resin hardens, but leaves a tacky residue requiring the application of the hot coat.

latitude. the distance measurement from the equator (north or south) calculated in degrees along a meridian line; each degree of latitude equals 60 nautical miles at that specific location.

launched. to be thrown into the air, usually caused by a wipeout.

layback. term used to describe a maneuver when a surfer lays back into the face of the wave as he progresses down the line; used to regulate speed or as an exhibition of style.

leash lag drag. when you wipe out and get dragged under water from your board as it is pulled through the soup; caused from having a leash that's too long or too short for the size of your board.

leash plug. a small, cylindrical plug with a metal rod used to attach a leash to a surfboard; inserted into the deck (top) near the tail of the board.

leash. a piece of surgical or similar tubing attaching the board to the rider's ankle (shortboard) or calf, just below the knee (longboard).

ledge. a part of an underwater land or coral mass that causes waves from deep water to jack and pitch forward when they hit it.

leggie. Australian term for a leash, shackle, leg rope, kook cord, etc.

leeward. converse application of windward; spot, area, side sheltered, or otherwise away from prevailing wind direction.

left. description for a breaking wave peeling to the left; left/right is always stated from the surfer's perspective facing toward shore or with back facing the wave.

length. a term used to describe the surfboard dimension as measured from nose to tail along the stringer.

licked. another term used to describe being worked, rag dolled, etc.

lifestyle. often the catch-all used by non-surfers to describe the way surfers go about living; "It's not a sport, it's a lifestyle."

light it up. a descriptive phrase use to describe a surfer who is surfing really well. they are said to be "lighting it up."

lines. description of waves approaching from the horizon.

lineup. place in the water just outside of where the waves break; where surfers line up to catch waves.

lip. the top of the face of the wave; usually curling forward as the wave breaks.

liquid smoke. the spray that comes off the back of a wave in an offshore wind; feathering; looks like smoke from a distance; "It's sick mate, liquid smoke everywhere."

locals. those who regularly surf at a particular surf spot or area; locals may or may not live at or near the spot, but their regular sessions mean they are accepted by the local surfing community.

locked in. to occupy the optimum position on the wave; trim; to maximize a ride.

log. a longboard that is nine feet or longer; characterized by generally thicker volume in the deck and rail areas; also tends to be fuller in volume with a spoon shaped nose.

long period swell. conditions caused by low pressure systems; more powerful and substantially bigger potential for size exists than with a trace swell.

longboard. usually more than 9' in length; their size makes them easier to paddle and allows the rider to get into waves earlier.

longshore current. water movement located in the surf zone that runs parallel to the shore as a result of waves breaking at an angle to the shoreline. can also be called littoral current.

long-sleeve spring. just what the term says…a spring suit (shorty) with long sleeves.

longitude. the distance from the prime meridian (east or west), from Greenwich, England as measured in degrees along a line; each meridian line runs in a north-south direction and starts/ends at the north/south poles.

loot. term used to describe surf gear or money used in buying surf gear.

losin' my religion. idiomatic expression of complete and utter exasperation; "I'm losin' my religion over this flat spell."

low pressure. an area of a relative pressure minimum that has converging winds and rotates in the same direction as the earth, counterclockwise in the northern hemisphere and clockwise in the southern hemisphere; stormy weather is often associated with low-pressure systems.

lull. relatively calm period between a set of waves.

M

mack. to eat without inhibition, usually after a surf session; also used to describe incredibly big waves, as in "That was s a macker!"

macking. a description used by surfers to describe the effect of a huge wave as it rolls through a lineup; it quite literally translates to being like a "mack truck" mowing something down.

make a wave. to go for a wave and make it as opposed to getting tossed off your board and pounded.

malibu. the name of a longboard in most places except the US; originated in California.

man in the gray suit. the term surfers in Australia use for a shark, you know, those Great White ones? "When I was out in the lineup I saw the Man in the Grey Suit go underneath me." California. "the landlord."

McFlip. a move that was developed by a locally famous surfer in Indialantic, FL at a spot called Two Roads (Uluwaturoads, Imperial Suites) that was developed when nobody else was watching; a maneuver that entails a full flip and a 360-degree mid-air turn that has yet to be seen by many others except for locals; No residing in San Diego, CA this maneuver has never been perfected by anyone else.

meter. unit of measure equal to 3.28 feet.

micro-mini. a perfectly shaped wave that is generally found breaking right onshore; too small to surf, but still contains all the classic elements of a good wave.

mid coast. term used to describe the area of surf breaks between Christies Beach and Moana.

mini-Malibu. the name of mid size board with longboard characteristics; old school.

mini gun. surfboard design credited to Dick Brewer of Hawaii around 1968 that featured the first signs of the modern outline; characterized by a narrower tail and pin-shaped nose.

moldy. term used for a type of surfboard manufacturing in which a hard plastic molded shell is injected with expanding foam; currently and most notably used by Bic surfboard manufacturers.

muku. the side of a wave near the crest; broken section of a wave; or, a wave to the left (see lala).

multi-suck. similar to a double-up, but much more intense; occurs when a double-up approaches a strong outflow or rebounding of water from waves that have already broken and are receding.

mushy. slow, sloppy waves of little or no power; better for a longboard.

N

nads. used to describe an unusually large burst of adrenaline that causes one to do something most would consider insane; "That wave was huge and your take-off was so late; you have got some serious nads."

nannobender. banana hammock, marble bag, banana bender, sausage sack; mostly worn by swimmers and muscle beach kooks who grease up and do not surf; occasionally you'll see some barney wearing them in the surf and this is a serious violation.

neap tide. a tide that occurs when the difference between high and low tide is least; the lowest level of high tide; neap tide comes twice a month, in the first and third quarters of the moon.

neoprene. material a wetsuit is made of; rubber.

nip-nash. term used to describe aggravated nipples from not wearing a rash guard or shirt.

nipped. nipples irritated and rubbed raw by board, wax or suit. a.k.a. tit rash.

nix. to quit, call-off or forgo.

no ka pakaka ale. gliding on the surf; probably refers mainly to canoe surfing; ohu; one of two kinds of surf ridden (the other is Lauloa); a low, small wave that rises without breaking but with enough strength to carry a board; sometimes called opuu.

nocty. ugly, nasty; "That girl is lookin nocty."

noodled. when a surfer's arms are exhausted; overall condition of a tired surfer.

nor'easter. a winter hurricane, generating large volumes of snow, high surf and tides, with a prevailing wind direction as its name implies.

North Shore. in the surf scene, this is the area on the north side of Oahu in Hawaii. this area is probably most notable for being the home shore of breaks like Pipeline, Sunset and some of the other heaviest, most dangerous breaks in the world.

nose. tip of a surfboard; the first 12" or so.

nose guard. soft rubber covering applied to surfboard nose to prevent a surfer from being skewered if hit.

nose ride. what is done when standing on the nose of a surfboard; only viable on a longboard.

nose width. a measurement from rail-to-rail, 12" back from the tip of the nose.

nosh. good; gnarly; sick; can be used for anything good, cool, fun; "Dude, she totally noshed that wave!" "What is up, honey? I'm noshin', you know."

O

o-town. another name for inland surfers in Orlando; mainland, or kooks from the mainland who normally play at rodeos but come to the coast on the weekends; some rip, most do not.

offshore. wind blowing from land toward the ocean; also used to describe surf conditions.

old school. pertaining something that has been done for some time; the style of legendary surfers is a good reference to old school.

olo. a type of surfboard, 16 to 18 feet in length and made of koa or wiliwili wood; used by Hawaiian royalty to surf prior to their overthrow in the late 19th century; hollow board which was the basis for the designs of Tom Blake.

onions. round circular dings in a surfboard that are usually caused by an impact from something or someone that is blunt. so named because they resemble the layers of an onion cut on cross section.

onshore. wind blowing from the ocean onto land.

opuu. Hawaiian term for extremely large and powerful swell; typical of a long-period swell.

orbitsville. to launch off the lip to land on the back of the wave.

oscillatory wave. a wave that travels forward while the water remains stationary; the wave orbits close as one complete wave passes; most waves are not purely oscillatory; a small forward movement of the water that is referred to as wave drift or mass transport.

outline. elliptical shape along the outer edge of a surfboard from the nose to the tail.

outside. refers to where you are in the line-up, or a place relative to the break; outside would be on the back of the breaking waves.

over the falls. taking a journey with the breaking wave and getting worked; generally caused by getting pulled back over the lip of a breaking wave; not a good thing!

overamped. a sure sign you need to switch to decaf; an overabundance of misguided energy.

overhead. wave heights that are greater than the height of the surfer riding the wave; often used as a measurement of the scale of waves such as: two feet overhead, three feet overhead, double overhead, triple overhead, etc.

oxygen debt. term used to describe what a surfer experiences after getting badly worked or enduring a really long hold-down; characterized by a burning sensation in the lungs.

Oz. abbreviated slang/lingo term used for a reference to Australia.

P

PWC. personal Water Craft; jet ski.

paipoboard. Hawaiian wooden bodyboard; old school, but still in use today.

papa hee nalu. a surfboard; literally, a board for sliding waves; translation: To give with the understanding the board will be returned.

park it. when a surfer slows his/her surfboard by bragging their trailing foot to position themselves in pocket of a peeling, throwing bomb in order to catch time in the green room, pit, barrel, etc.

park off. veg-out; when you park off, you just plain relax.

party wave. a large enough wave to accommodate several surfers at once.

peak period. the period of time during a weather event when the most energy of a swell hits a specific area.

peak. the hump in the middle of an approaching wave; becomes more prominent as it starts to hit more shallow water and defines which way a surfer should go; frontside or backside.

peaky lines. a really wide wave that enables a surfer to take off at any of the peaks and usually get some sort of ride before the wave breaks into smaller sections.

pearl. when the nose of the surfboard is buried underwater on a drop-in/take off; usually precedes a wipe out.

pearlitis. a condition by which a surfer pearls continuously, generally resulting in the surfer being worked or rag dolled.

peelin'. a condition in which a wave breaks perfectly from takeoff all the way down the line and "peels" as it moves from start to finish.

period. time interval between waves; wind swell less than 10 seconds; 12 seconds and longer is typically considered ground swell; the energy/power of a wave is proportional not only to its height but its period.

pet the cat. the act of surfing down the line of a breaking wave face while dragging ones hand on its face.

phazer bottom. dimple-bottom design introduced by the Willis bros, Milton and Michael, on the north shore of Oahu in the early 80s; the design went on to set speed records in the wind boarding world and influenced wake board and boogie board bottom designs.

pig dog. Australian term meaning getting barreled while dragging a hand, hip or a butt cheek in the water to modulate one's speed.

pilot. term used when referring to a jet ski driver who tows surfers into huge waves.

pintail. a pointed tail that aids in stability of surfboard; usually found on guns and best when used in very large surf.

Pipeline, Pipe, Banzai Pipeline. Banzai, a rallying cry used by Japanese warriors through the conclusion of the Second World War; the last north Shore Oahu spot to be ridden; commonly known as pipe because of its perfect, hollow shaped tube; first ridden in 1967 by Phil Edwards.

pit. place directly in front of the crest of the wave; the hollow part of a breaking wave beneath the pitching lip.

pitted. to get tubed; to spend time in the green room; tucked in the womb; it's all good.

pitch. description of a breaking wave's action as it builds up, and breaks.

pitched. tossed off the lip of the wave and usually off your board.

pitchpole. when you pearl and go over the nose as the board flips behind you as the wave closes out on you and you get worked.

plank. another name for a longboard; any surfboard greater than 9 feet in length.

platter. a surfboard that is in the fun board genre; usually 7 to 8.5 feet, wider than a regular shortboard, and has some longboard and some 70s style fish characteristics; can have any type of tail from a swallow, pin, square, or squash; most seem to be rounded pin tails or rounded squash tails.

plug. a shaped blank produced by a top designer as a template for a computer shaping machine (CAD/CAM); also a similarly crafted shape supplied by a designer to a blank manufacturer as a basis for blank molding.

plunger. someone who constantly pearls or plunges straight into the water and lets their board shoot straight out of the water.

plunging waves. a setup where waves wrap around a point of land creating perfectly lined up, peeling waves.

point break. a wave that forms in reaction to a land form jutting toward the sea; consistent, hollow and generally a long ride.

polyester. a type of plastic resin; the most common type used in surfboard manufacturing; not your g-daddy's slacks.

polystyrene. a type of plastic foam used to make surfboard blanks, usually employed together with epoxy resins.

polyurethane. a type of plastic foam that is most commonly used in surfboard manufacturing when polyester resin is used.

pop shuv-it. a maneuver that is similar to a chop hop with the difference being that the surfer spins the surfboard 180-degrees under their feet while they are in the air.

pop, pop up. the action a surfer uses to get to a standing position on a surfboard.

prone out. to drop to your belly after riding a wave; usually done when a surfer is coming in after a session; maneuver which lowers and dispersers a surfers weight and center of gravity making riding the whitewater all the way to the beach easier.

poser. a non-surfer playing the role of a surfer; a Kook.

pounded. to be held under a substantial amount of time while being washed around by a wave; hold down.

posuer. wanna-be surfer who dresses the part, but is really clueless about surfing; nice baggies brah!

prevailing wind. a wind that blows from a given direction more frequently than any other during a given time period, such as a day, month, season, or year.

prone. to ride with your belly on the board; position taken on a body board.

propagate. the technical term used to define the movement of swell/waves across the ocean; swell and waves "propagate" from a weather event toward other areas.

pruned. condition where the fingers become ill-shaped after a long period of time in the water.

pucker. the factor used to measure the effect an intimidating wave has on ones ability to remain calm and collected.

punt. the Australian term for launching into an air maneuver.

pull off. to succeed making a radical maneuver; as in "I can't believe he pulled off that backside 360."

pumpin. from southern hemisphere surf lingo, pronounced p—aar—mpin' clean and powerful waves; 4ft plus. goin' off; sick.

punchy. term used in Australia to describe the wave's level of power; powerful waves are really punchy as opposed to slop, which is slow and weak.

pure sex. something that is awesome is described as being that of "pure sex;" "The surf today was pure sex."

Q

quad. Four-fin board, two normal size fins with two smaller fins in line behind them.

quiver. an individual collection of specialized surfboards; a board bag that holds several boards; term used to describe what one brought to surf with.

R

racy. term used to describe a really fast wave or section of a wave.

radical. departure from the ordinary; revolutionary, abrupt; coined by long-boarders of the golden era to define positive energy, great design, superior conditions, and great ridesmanship.

rag dolled. to get drilled, rolled and tumbled by a breaking wave.

rail 50/50. antiquated shape whereby rails are of equal proportions or dimensional characteristics, top and bottom of the surfboard.

rail grab. the act of holding onto the rail of a surfboard to maintain control during a maneuver; most commonly used in backside tube riding (see "pigdog"), but also used when pulling aerials.

rail sandwich. event precipitated by going over the falls and having the surfboard find its way between the riders legs with impunity.

rail, boxy. full, thick, or heavy rail; clearly defined rounded corners, with very little tapering; design application best for smaller wave riding; found today mostly on hybrid type boards or conventional boards shaped for taller heavier riders.

rail, full. standard shortboard rail; tapering from board center to the rail is more pronounced than the boxy rail, but reflects similar rounded corners.

rail, thin. shape application for larger waves with a hollow shape; well-defined tapering to a narrow and thoroughly rounded edge; well-suited to the lean rider.

rail. the outside edge of a surfboard.

rake. the distance between the back edge of the fin base and the tip of the fin, measured down the length of a surfboard.

random stander. inexperienced surfer or someone who only surfs on weekends or when their wife lets them; please, get a pair.

rashguard. spandex shirt used in surfing to prevent a rash.

rebound. action of a wave refracting off of a jetty, pier or other immovable object that bounces it in another direction.

reef break. waves that form over an underwater reef or rock, very consistent, but can be somewhat dangerous, especially if you get caught inside.

reef cut. scratches, abrasions, or gashes from a reef.

reek. a really sour smell; can be used to describe anything from dead sea life to the stank a brah emits after eating a gas station burrito.

reentry. attacking the lip, usually going vertically and then turning nose down and re-entering the wave.

reflect. the occurrence in which a wave rebounds off a hard object (seawall, jetty, etc.) and combines with the original wave.

refraction. the occurrence when a wave bends as it drags over the bottom or an uneven ocean floor.

regular foot. a surfer who surfs with his/her left foot forward and faces the wave on rights; also called a "natural foot" in oz.

release. the effect that allows water to be accelerated as it passes along the surfboard surfaces; most noticeable in the tail section of the board, through tail rocker, outline curves, trailing fin (center) edge, and bottom.

resin. a liquid plastic that hardens when mixed with a catalyst (methyl ethyl ketone); used primarily in surfboard manufacturing to seal the shaped blank and to repair major dings or creases.

respect. what you should always have for the sea, the waves, nature and everyone in the line-up.

reverse. to spin 180-degrees and surf backwards with the nose of the board in the trailing direction; generally only done as a finishing maneuver.

reverse. hard chine protruding ridge on the bottom of the surfboard running the length of it.

reverse vee. surfboard bottom contour credited to Maurice Cole of oz, in which the "vee" is in the front half of the board; this idea revolutionized the traditional mindset of surfboard characteristics; reverse vee, also known as "revee" or forward vee, is common used today, especially in big-wave boards.

rhino. a board for big waves they are long, narrow, and pointy both at the nose and the tail for maximum rail contact; usually thick and heavy and ranging in length from 7' to 10' e.g. elephant gun, rhino chaser.

rickt. derived from off the Richter scale; replacement for sweet, killer, cool, epic; "My go-out was rickt today!"

rig. a complete compliment of necessary surf gear; a jet ski or surf vehicle fully kitted-out is a "rig."

righteous. totally awesome, of the chain, term used when describing an action, object, idea, or person; "That's so 'righteous' dude!"

rip tide. ocean flow characterized by strong out-flowing current.

rip. to surf to the best of abilities; also used to define a condition of the water, especially when citing it relative to the current.

ripper. someone who rips or shreds at surfing; someone who surfs exceptionally well.

ripping. executing drastic and radical moves on the wave; having it your way with a wave.

riprocked. term used to describe when you get your second wind; a refreshed feeling.

river mouth. a wave that forms on the sediments deposited at a river mouth; similar to beach breaks but sometimes more susceptible to being sectiony.

rocker. the curve along the bottom of the surfboard from nose to tail; accelerated rocker increased curve in the rocker in a relatively short distance; the arc of the tail that bends up, more rocker = easier turning & less speed.

room. inside the barrel; synonymous with green room.

roundtail. a tail shape in which the two sides of the board come together in smooth curves to form a semi-circle; a rounded-tail block.

rubbered. the condition or feeling of a surfers arms after having completed a day long session.

S

sane. a term coined by a surfer in satellite beach, Florida when someone did something outrageous, or a very intense maneuver or trick; "That off the lip was sane!" Gregory Lee Smith, who coined this phrase, died at the age of 49 on Christmas eve of 2003. His surf lingo will live on in the Brevard County and San Diego beaches forever.

sausage sling. another term for banana hammocks, nannobenders, marble bags; derived primarily from sausage sack it is a forbidden piece of attire in the surfing world that is primarily used by members of muscle beach, swimmers, non-surfers, or your average beer gut friend frolicking in the water in pacific beach; "Look at that guy in the sausage sling! scary!!"

sausagefest. many barnyards in the water at once; when there are many kooks in the water there is a "sausagefest" going on out there; Pacific Beach is known for this on a daily basis.

scab. a reef or rock; usually associated with reef or point breaks that are shallow.

scattered peaks. a condition in which waves break apart into different peaks/ lines with a clear separation between the wave shoulders.

schlong. thick, long old school surfboard; term was also used to describe someone who rode one; way out of date, bruddah!

schnot shot. the process of alternately plugging a nostril and blowing out in an attempt to eject seawater from ones sinus cavity after being worked by a bomb or getting rag dolled.

score. to acquire, gain or achieve; "Scored a some great rides today."

scraps. description for the type of waves that some surfers ride on the inside section. also known as crumbs or crumb beaters.

sea lice. jellyfish larvae that embed themselves in your skin causing an annoying itch and sometimes a nasty rash; especially bad in the spring.

sea smoke. the condensing of moisture to the point that water vapor becomes so condensed that the combined molecules become visible to the naked eye; the occurrence when cold air passes over a warm body of water or warm air over a cold body of water.

sea state. the term used to define the present condition or state of the sea.

seal skin. a really thick or heavy wet suit; usually 5mm or more.

section. a part of a wave that breaks out of sequence from the peeling face; also used to describe areas of several waves that form individual peaks that break independently from the main part of a breaking wave.

seine waves. deep water swells that are very well-approximated by pure sine waves; steep—refers to angle or pitch of wave face; waves formed close to the shore by local wind conditions, unorganized, tendency to be slop.

set. a group of approaching waves; generated offshore by surface winds that propagate toward land.

setup. a general moniker used to describe a surf break; it includes topography, bathymetry ocean floor contour, land mass points, etc. and sandbars; also used as a general description; "The setup was so awesome for the swell…it just wrapped around the point." also used to describe surfboard characteristics.

shacked. to get tubed; barreled; spend time in the green room; as in "Dude you got frickin' shacked on that last wave."

shaka, shaka brah. Hawaiian pidgin for "right on!"; also a hand signal surfers use for "Howzit?"; incorrectly believed to mean hang loose; performed by extending the thumb and pinky with a slight wiggle.

shallows. a moniker used for the description of water that is less than one-half the wavelength (distance between wave crests).

shape. a surfboard's outline; also known as template; act of shaping a surfboard.

shaper. the surfboard maker who planes and sands a blank to the desired shape prior to glassing; requires incredible skill, patience and experience.

shifty peak. moniker for occurrence when inconsistent swell direction or differing bathymetry causes waves to break in different locations across a spot; most notable in windy conditions.

shoaling. the result of waves slowing down from friction as they begin to drag across the ocean floor.

shockwave. Effect out-flowing water or an uneven bottom has on clean, peeling wave face as it moves forward; causes a "shockwave" effect as the face buckles slightly; generally only felt/seen by surfers when riding exceptionally clean, hollow waves; sometimes referred to as "steps."

shoobie. originally coined by folks on the east coast from Atlantic City, NJ, in reference to people from Philly carrying their belongings to the beach in a shoe box; an out of towner who would bring their lunches in shoe boxes to the shore; also commonly called a barney.

shooter. an Australian term for a surfboard.

shoot the curl. an outdated term used when a surfer trims his/her board at the curl of the wave.

shore break. waves break very close to the beach; generally closeouts.

shore dump. unorganized sloppy foam, not good for surfing.

shortboard. most common surfboard ranging from 5' to 7'6", and tend to be used for high-performance contest-style surfing; a shortboard usually has a pointed nose and three fins, although other configurations are common; a shortboard sacrifices paddling and floatation for the sake of performance.

shoulder hopper. a person who tends to sit outside the lineup and catch the soft, mushy portion of a breaking wave.

shoulder ride. a fairly straight, benign ride in the pocket or the critical section between the pitching lip and the wave face.

shove-it. when a surfer performs an aerial maneuver, spins the board 180-degrees landing on it backwards, and rides out in the opposite stance to what they were riding before starting the move.

shred. ability to execute rapid repeated turns; shortboard term.

shubee. a tourist who buys surfing gear, dresses surf, but has never surfed in their life.

shweet. something that is really cool, awesome or appreciated.

sick. excellent, top notch—describing a surfer, stunt, maneuver or conditions.

sideshore. breeze blowing parallel to the coastline; also used to describe conditions.

sideslip. action of a surfboard when it stops tracking forward and moves sideways.

sinus drain. what happens when water drains out of the sinus cavity that has collected from being worked during a previous go out.

Six-feet, offshore. description of ideal conditions when a brah/wahine calls up at 5 a.m. and asks; Howzit?.

skeg. variant of nautical term being section of keel of a ship to the sternpost; applied by longboard shapers to a single fin setup, permanently glassed to the surfboard.

sketchy. not a sure thing; possibility something will not occur as anticipated or desired; also used to describe conditions.

skimboard. glassed plywood or fiberglassed board for riding shallow beaches on the water's edge.

skurfing. the morphed aquatic activity of riding a surfboard, while being towed behind a boat or PWC in the same manner as water skiing.

slab. an extremely hollow thick wave; really gnarly; think Tavarua, Fiji.

slack tide. term used to describe dead-low tide or condition where the influence of the moons gravitational pull is seen least.

slam. to bounce off the lip as it begins to pitch.

slammed. when a wave comes down hard and knocks you off hard.

slap down. the sound the front of the surfboard makes when it slaps down as you paddle out and a wave rolls underneath you.

slash. a radical, carving cutback performed on the face of the wave.

slingshot. a word to describe the effect of a rebounding wave off of a jetty that refracts in another direction; when a surfer paddles into a wave like this and makes the drop he/she is propelled down the line with great speed; Sebastian Inlet's first peak has a perfect slingshot when there is a good south swell.

slop. crappy surf; also used to describe conditions in general and the condition (power) of the prevailing swell.

slushy. a person who only rides the foam of the wave (whitewater) with a surfboard after it closes out.

snake. to paddle around behind someone who is in position and steal their wave; not a good thing.

snap. riding up the face of the wave and executing a hard, crisp 180 off the lip and leading down the face of the wave to setup a subsequent maneuver.

snapback. a quick, short cutback into the power of the wave; often used in a steep part of the wave when the quick maneuver will keep the surfer in the "power pocket" of the wave; used when the wave is too fast to offer a chance to do a full cutback because the wave would pass the surfer by.

sneaker set/sleeper set. an unusually large or rogue set of waves that usually catches the surfers in the lineup off guard or too far inside.

snip. this term is used when you have nothing better to say; 1)"What are you doing?" "I'm snippin'; "Yo, sniiiiiip!"; "Call me later so we can snip."

soft board. surfboard for beginners with a soft-top or deck constructed of a firm foam-like material; some older soft boards also have soft, but slick bottoms; much safer for beginners to use when learning as they are less likely to get hurt if the surfboard hits them.

soft rail. a rounded edge to a surfboard that allows the board to be loose in handling characteristics.

solid. adapted from musical slang; representing excellence, well performed, satisfying; longboard-era terminology.

soul arch. executed off a smooth bottom turn by shifting one's weight to the inside rail and sticking your belly out creating an arched back; a sweet form of art performed on a wave.

soul. an attitude, a feeling, a style of riding a wave, an also a way of approaching surf culture; anti competitive, environmentally friendly, respectful of history and the integrity of the wave itself; "Go with the flow, bro."

soup bowl. steep takeoff point with mushy shoulders on both sides; prevalent on the east coast of the US.

soup. the after-effects of a breaking brave; especially evident on a closesout; see also, whitewater.

spackled. when a surfer riding a wave cuts back or uses a maneuver to spray someone paddling back out to the lineup; same as "frosted."

spade, spadework. to date a member of the opposite sex; spadework is the act of dating someone with a specific purpose of…you fill in the blank.

spat out. when a surfer finishes a tube ride in a hollow wave and exits at the same time the compressed air within the tube is forced out in a mist of spray.

spilling waves. term generally used to describe a soft, mushy wave that is characterized by a gradually breaking crest as the wave travels to the shore.

spin cycle. wiping out and getting worked until you don't know which way is up.

spinner. longboard maneuver spinning the board 360-degrees by a process of removing the skag from the water, while standing on the nose, rotating the board, and returning to previous position.

spin out. situation when the fins break loose from the water causing a loss of control; usually occurs when a surfer turns too hard in a steep part of a wave, or if the surfer turned too hard when going over a bumpy section on a wave.

spit. the spraying of mist from the collapsing vortex of a wave.

sponge. called sponge because its core is made of a sponge-like material; a bodyboard.

sponger. a general moniker applied to someone who bodyboards.

spoon. concave underside of a longboard' s nose; also used to describe the nose shape of a surfboard; spoon is a more rounded shape.

spray. the fanning of water off of the top of the wave when it is peeling and the wind is straight offshore. also occurs when a surfer executes a heavy top turn or off-the-top.

spring tide. the exceptionally high and low tides that occur at the time of the new moon or the full moon when the sun, moon, and earth are approximately aligned.

square tail. tail block design of a surfboard whereby the tail is severely squared; old school...really old school; think redwood-planks-glued-together old.

squarepants spongekook. another name for a kook sponger; in the "nannobenders" genre in the fact that spongers can be ridiculed as much as one who wears nannobenders.

squash tail. tail block design of a surfboard whereby the tail is slightly squared; generally, just a few to several inches across the back.

squid lid. another name for a hood used for cold air or cold water in the winter.

squid. unlikable or disrespected person; a kook; also used to describe someone in the lineup who has little to no regard for fellow surfers.

squirly. the way a board wiggles as it is being pushed by particularly strong whitewater or as it nears the bottom of a steep wave; describes a board, usually a shortboard, with squirly action.

stainpile. another word for storm drain, tubed, bowled, shacked, or getting in the greenroom; someone will hoot "Stainpile" when you fly down the line, tuck in for a good tube, and come out dry.

stall. aeronautical term applied to surfing, whereby ones drags the back of the surfboard by a controlled weight shift; this is done to achieve a better position on the face of the wave or to get into the tube.

step off. maneuver used to kick the board clear of the breaking wave; flick off.

stick. your surf board; originated in the 80s and has been taken over by "board."

stinkbug stance. a description of a person with a very squatty stance where their butt almost hits the board and their feet are spread apart too wide for maneuverability or a good style to occur; coined in the original Endless Summer movie.

stink-eye. hard, cold, menacing stare; expression given by locals to outsiders.

stoke. condition of being geared, wound up, full of enthusiasm; as in, "I'm stoked, man! I just got tubed!"

stokerfade. when a surf trip ends without scoring waves it is said to be have been a "stokerfade."

stone zone. phrase used to describe someone well endowed with...courage; "Dude, that drop was so gnarly, you must be packing large in the "stone zone.""

storm surge. the abnormal rise in sea level accompanying a hurricane or other intense storm, caused primarily by the winds influence on the water; storm surges are greatly enhanced when the storm winds blow the water into partially land-locked areas like bays where the excess water can't escape; the measurement of the storm surge height is the difference between the actual observed sea level associated with the storm and the normal sea level that would have occurred without the storm; increased storm surge may also occur from the reduction of atmospheric pressure associated with the lower pressure in a storm or cyclone.

storm drain. yet another term for bowled, tubed, greenroom, or shacked; when paddling out you yell, "Storm drain!" when a guy is in an insane tube or especially critical situation on a wave.

storm warning. a warning issued by the national weather service when current or forecasted ocean surface wind speeds are sustained at 48 knots (55 mph) or greater in a specific area.

stormy. trashed surfing conditions with strong winds, large chop in the water, and generally accompanied by with rain, hail, snow, and/or lightning; overall a great time to find something else to do.

stringer. narrow strip or strips of hard wood running down the center of the surfboard; if multiple stringer design, more than one strip will run parallel from nose to tail.

stroppy. common term used to describe someone who is cheeky, an assmunch, jerk, haole, kook, etc.

strue bob. South African phrase meaning "I shit you not, strue bob, I caught a 50' bomb."

stuffed. to get barreled; "Rick got so stuffed on the last a-frame that I could not even see him;" getting driven under the water by a wave coming down on you; hold-down.

stylie. to perform a maneuver with good form; with style.

stylin'. to be dialed in. when everything clicks and you find yourself surfing like a pro.

subtropical air. an air mass that forms over the subtropical region; the air is typically warm with a high moisture content due to the low evaporative process.

subtropical cyclone. a low-pressure system generally located between 15- and 35-degrees latitude that has characteristics of both tropical and extra tropical cyclones; these generally short-lived systems may be either cold core or warm core.

subtropical depression. a subtropical cyclone in which the maximum sustained surface wind speeds are less than 33 knots (38 mph).

subtropical storm. a subtropical cyclone in which the maximum sustained surface wind speeds are greater than 34 knots (39 mph).

sucked dry. a wave that really jacks up leaving the water in front of it very shallow; generally occurs over reef, but can occur anywhere there is a strong swell.

superman. an air maneuver performed when a surfer kicks out their legs while holding onto their board.

surfari. a long-standing term used to describe a surf trip; originated in Africa, but generally applies to anyone traveling abroad for a surf trip safari.

surf beat. the rhythmic rise and fall in coastal water levels caused by sets of waves as they arrive and create a surge of water along a surf zone; during and immediately after a set of waves, the water level along the shore rises from the wave energy pushing water ashore. once the sets of waves cease or lull, the water will escape back out to deep water-sometimes in the form of rip currents or rip tides before another set of waves arrive to complete the cycle called the surf beat.

surf height. the measurement of breaking waves along the coast; Surfline measures wave heights by the face of the wave for consistency in communication; when communicating we also compare wave heights to a surfer's body height. figuring a surfer averages 5 feet tall when semi crouching and surfing a wave. 1 foot = ankle high; 2 feet = knee high; 3 feet = waist high; 4 feet = chest high; 5 feet = head high; 1 foot overhead = 6 feet; 2 feet overhead = 7 feet, etc.; 10 feet = double overhead; 15 feet = triple overhead, etc. note. Hawaiians and a few other areas throughout the world measure waves by the back of the wave and they estimate the waves' backs to be one half of the wave face height. the Hawaiian's intent is probably to stay consistent with the deep-water swell height of the waves before they began to shoal, as compared to the wave heights on buoy 51001 located nm of Kuai. however, this procedure is inherently flawed because numerous variables like swell period, refraction, and shoaling can greatly alter the transition of deep-water swell to breaking waves by 1.5 times to 5 times the original deep-water swell height.

surf zone. the area along the coast where there are breaking waves and lines of whitewater moving shoreward toward shallower water and the shore; may also include an offshore deepwater reef where there are breaking waves and whitewater.

surfboard channel. bottom shape originating during the 1970s, credited to Jim Pollard of oz, in which grooves were cut along the surfboard (parallel to stringer), usually through the tail half; many different types of channels have a variety of effects on performance; generally they add drive and directional stability.

Surfer's ear. when long-term exposure to cold water and wind leads to an enlargement of the bone in the inner ear canal.

surfer's knots. large bumps on the top of a surfers foot and on knees caused by callusing.

surfer's lung. the inability of some to breathe deep due to a long day of getting worked and inhaling mostly salt water.

surfspeak. term used to describe the medium of exchange between members of the surfing sub-culture.

surging waves. a scientific term to describe waves that don't have time to break because the transition from deep-water to shallow water is too fast. very little white water is evident before surging waves reach the shore; typically happens in many areas during high tide.

swallow tail. tail block design; a double-pointed tail with an indentation in the center; adds to the surfboard's holding ability.

sweet spot. the place where a surfer places his/her feet for maximum balance, stability and maneuverability.

swell train. term used by oceanographers to describe swells radiating from the center of ocean storms; where they go, how big they get and when they'll arrive at a given point.

swell. wind-generated waves that have traveled beyond their generating area, usually from a storm far out to sea. strong winds in a storm will transfer wind energy into the water, which will create waves. as the waves grow larger with continued wind, the energy will transfer deeper below the ocean surface. as the waves move out of the storm area, the stronger waves with more energy below the ocean surface will maintain their strength over distance and will be characterized as deep water waves or swell; termed as the significant wave event arriving at a surfing location created by a storm out to sea, as all of the waves from the storm arrive over a period of time consisting of hours or extending over days; wave energy in deeper water before the waves begin to shoal over shallow water and break.

swell direction. where the swell is coming from; in the marine community, swell direction is always identified from the swell source, not its destination; see direction.

swell height. the average height of the highest one-third of the swells with swell period energies over 11 seconds; shorter-period wind wave energy with periods under 11 seconds is excluded.

swell period. the peak period of the swell energy in seconds; if there are multiple swells at a specific location, then the peak period of the dominant swell is used; this is the time between successive wave crests as they pass a stationary point on the ocean surface, such as a buoy.

swell shadow. the area behind islands, points of land, or other obstacles where the swell and waves have been blocked by those obstacles; the swell shadow will change with different swell directions.

swell window. the opening through which swell and waves may pass between islands or around points of land; the swell window will change with different swell directions.

swish. a surfer who is either meek or fearful…or both.

switch stance. description of what a switch-foot does; signifies an accomplished surfer; not easy to do.

switch-foot. a surfer who is equally adept and going regular or goofy foot depending one the way the wave breaks.

T

table de surf. French term for a surfboard; mainstream in France when using native tongue.

tail. back or trailing portion of a surfboard.

tail block. very end or tail of a surfboard; preface to description when a surfer is explaining a surfboard characteristic.

tail kick. the amount of increase in the rate of rocker near the tail

tail pad. a surface patch made of neoprene or similar substance to assist surfers in maintaining traction with their board; most often used for rear foot (tail) positions, but can also be used at the forefoot position.

tail slide. part of a larger maneuver in which the surfer purposely makes his/her fins lose their grip and the board slides.

tail width. a measurement from the rail-to-rail 12" from the tail.

takeoff. the best spot to be in the line-up to catch the best part of a breaking wave.

talk story. the reciting of tales related to ones surfing experiences; when a crew gets together this can be quite an entertaining event; surfers are not known to be tellers of "fish stories", so they're probably at least loosely interpretable as fact…at least in their view.

tanker. the same as log; term for a long, heavy surfboard.

template. a wooden sheet cut into an imaginary surfboard curve, used by a shaper or designer to draw outlines onto a blank prior to shaping; made of thin plywood or plastic; the outline curve of one side of the template may be an outline for the nose of a surfboard, while the outline curve of the other side of the same template may be an outline for the tail section of the surfboard. surfboard shapers typically create their own templates and come in all sizes and shapes depending on the type of surfboard to be shaped; also used as a design term to describe which style of design was used to shape it; outline.

tertiary swell. the third dominant swell at a specific location; the primary swell is the dominant swell, followed by the secondary swell, followed by the tertiary swell.

thickness. a surfboard's dimension as measured from the deck to the bottom of the board.

thongs. old-school term from which the word slaps (US, TX) came in the 80s; flip-flops.

thrashed. occurrence when a wave pounds you; same as getting worked.

three-o. a 360-degree rotation…go figure.

throwin' heat. another phrase used for ripping; as in "Dude, you were throwin' some serious heat out there today."

throwing tail. sliding the tail of a surfboard in a turn, breaking the grip of the fins"

thruster. a surfboard with three similar size fins; also known as a tri-fin.

thursday night surf club. event where local crew hooks up for a late afternoon go out and some local cuisine; props to Mark.

toe in. pushing the front of the fins in. causing pressure on the outside of the fins to be greater than on the inside; makes the board want to respond to either side from surfer input; used to eliminate tracking of earlier twin fins.

toes-on-the-nose. riding a wave with your toes curled over the nose of the board; longboard maneuver.

tombstonein'. what happens when you get held down so deep that your leash is pulling your board under vertically so that only the tip is bobbing up and down above the surface of the water.

top turn. similar to the re-entry but the approach is less vertical and usually performed to gain speed.

tow board. a surfboard designed specifically to be used for tow-in surfing; usually features foot straps to assist the surfer in maintaining control in larger surf.

tow in. being towed into waves by boat or PWC that are too large to paddle into.

trace. term used to describe a slight, weak swell that is almost unnoticeable until it reaches very shallow water; caused by surface winds, as opposed to long period swell which is caused by low pressure systems.

traction pad. rubber/foam pad applied to tail of a surfboard to assist the surfer in maintaining contact with the surfboard.

trade winds. two belts of prevailing winds that blow easterly from the subtropical high pressure centers toward the equatorial trough; primarily lower level winds, they are characterized by their great consistency of direction. in the northern hemisphere, the trades blow from the northeast, and in the southern hemisphere, the trades blow from the southeast.

translatory wave. a wave in which both the wave form and water move forward; a breaking wave is considered to be in "translatory" state as the water particles are significantly projected forward with the wave.

tri fin. a three-fin surfboard; one large and two smaller fins.

trim. adjusting your position on a board so that it planes, and achieves maximum speed.

tropical cyclone. a warm-core cyclone, originating over tropical or subtropical waters, with a closed surface wind circulation around a well-defined center. the associated maximum sustained surface wind speed will range from 34 knots to 63 knots (39 to 73 mph). ocean water temperatures need to be at least 80 degrees Fahrenheit to maintain the development of the cyclone, which is the extraction of heat energy from the ocean and heat export at the low temperatures of the upper troposphere.

tropical depression or disturbance. a warm-core cyclone, originating over tropical or subtropical waters, in which the maximum sustained surface wind speed, is 33 knots (38 mph) or less.

tropical storm warning. a warning issued by the national hurricane center that winds within the range of 34 to 63 knots (39 to 73 mph) associated with a tropical cyclone are expected in a specified coastal area within 24 hours or less.

tropical storm watch. an announcement for specific coastal areas that tropical storm conditions are possible within 36 hours.

tropical wave. a trough, disturbance, or cyclonic curvature in the trade-wind easterlies originating over tropical or subtropical waters; tropical waves are the first sign of possible tropical cyclone development.

trough. the lowest part of a wave as it begins to break; in deep water, the middle or lowest area between two wave crests.

tsunami. commonly (and incorrectly) known as a tidal wave, a tsunami involves long period ocean waves generated by earthquakes and other geological or tectonic disturbances below sea level. tsunamis can travel at speeds of up to 500 knots through the open ocean. while they may be of low height in deep water, the shoaling process as they approach land can increase the tsunami to heights of over 35 feet or more in bays or other restricted areas.

trunkable. term used to denote the ocean water temperature as being warm enough for one to shed the rubber (wetsuit) and surf in trunks alone.

tube. the cylindrical vortex or cone shaped hole created when the lip pitches out far and clean enough to create a space between the wave and the falls.

tubeage. another word for tubed, barreled, green room, shacked, or bowled.

tubed. riding inside the tube; in the green room.

tube ride. where the surfer rides behind or inside the broken curl of the wave; also known as "in the barrel."

turn turtle. method of going under waves for longboarders; used instead of duck diving...which is really impossible with a longboard.

twin. term used to describe a style of two fin surfboard. old school.

twinzer. a four-fin surfboard; two normal size fins with two smaller fins a few inches outside and forward.

U

unreal. term used to describe something that is beyond what one generally expects.

upwelling. the process by which water rises from a lower to a higher depth, usually as a result of divergence and offshore currents. it influences climate by bringing colder, more nutrient-rich water to the surface; a vital factor of the el nino event.

utopic. condition arising from pulling up to a secret spot and finding it 5'–10', offshore and glassy; derivation of epic.

V

varial. a shove-it with the difference being that a surfer spins the surfboard with their hand.

vaycay. an awesome vacation! "Dude! this trip's been a total vaycay!"

vee bottom. similar to boat hull design; bottom tapering to a subtle angle; allows the rider easier access to putting the board on the rail.

vee. a bottom shape in which the stringer is lower than the rails when viewed from the side; originated in the tail area during the late 1960s by oz designer Bob McTavish and several contemporaries. tail vee was a design standard until the early 1990s, when experiments with concaves and reverse vee (see "reverse vee") virtually eliminated it from small wave equipment; still the preferred bottom contour in many medium to large wave boards.

velocity. the strength that wind blows in a swell generation event; also one of the central tenets in wave generation along with duration and fetch.

Velzyland. legendary Hawaiian spot named in honor of legendary shaper/rider Dale Velzy; props to Bruce Brown and others…

vertical. to turn and head straight up the wave face.

victory-at-sea. blown out, stormy, mixed up surf conditions or just plain "victory."

volume. the total buoyancy of the surfboard; floatability.

W

waffling. rapidly tracking the surfboard back and forth.

wahine. Hawaiian term used as a moniker for women surfers; term is also used by bruddah surfers to refer to their counterparts of the opposite gender; term of affection.

Waimea. a Hawaiian bay that receives huge swell; first ridden in 1957.

wannabe. description of someone who wants to be a surfer who dresses the part, and has the gear but cannot pull it off.

warm front. a warm front is the leading edge of an advancing warm air mass that is replacing a retreating relatively colder air mass. generally, with the passage of a warm front, the temperature and humidity increase, the pressure rises, and although the wind shifts (usually from the southwest to the northwest in the northern hemisphere), it is not as pronounced as with a cold frontal passage. precipitation, in the form of rain, snow, or drizzle, is generally found ahead of the surface front, as well as convective showers and thunderstorms. fog is common in the cold air ahead of the front. although clearing usually occurs after passage, some conditions may produce fog in the warm air.

washing machine. when prevailing surf conditions resemble the form of a load of laundry as it is being agitated.

wave decay. as waves move out of the storm area where they were created, they decrease greatly in size within the first thousand miles (more than 60 percent) and slowly thereafter; caused by three factors: short-period waves and chop dissipating rapidly once outside of the wind-generation area; directional spreading of waves as they move away from the storm at different angles; and the separation of waves as they travel forward at different speeds after leaving the storm area.

wave height. the vertical distance between a wave crest and the trough.

wave length. the distance between successive wave crests.

wave period. the time in seconds between successive wave crests as they pass a stationary point on the ocean surface, such as a buoy.

wave spectrum. the mathematical equation showing the distribution of wave energy in the different wave frequencies or wave periods. by analyzing the wave spectrum with LOLA, Surfline forecasters are able to separate the wave trains at a specific location like a buoy or a point on a swell model. this allows us to filter out unimportant wave and swell energy, so we can isolate the important wave and swell energy, which will greatly affect the accuracy of the surf forecast for a specific location.

wave steepness. the ratio of the wave height to the wavelength; a term used by the national data buoy center (NDBC) to describe the dominant sea state at a buoy. for a given wave height, steep waves represent a more serious threat to capsizing vessels or damaging marine structures than broad swell.

wave-group velocity. the forward speed of a swell or a set of waves is equal to 1.5 times the period between successive waves in the group. the waves within a group travel at twice the speed as the overall group (3 times the swell period). for example; if a swell has a period of 10 seconds, individual waves will be moving at 30 knots, while the group as a whole will be moving forward at 15 knots. as each wave travels forward within the group and reaches the front, it will fall back to the rear to repeat the cycle.

wave hog. a surfer that catches the majority of waves during any given session; an experienced, well-conditioned, motivated and skillful surfer; usually applies to longboarders; a non-endearing term from one surfer to another, when accused wave hog is having a righteous day of ripping and taking all the biggest and best waves.

wax bum. someone who sits on the beach with his or her board and never goes out, but just keeps waxing his/her board; wannabe.

wax. Paraffin; used on surfboard deck to prevent slipping.

way of life. semi-interchangeable with lifestyle; this is a more accurate definition for how surfers see the sport and life.

wedge. a wave condition in which two waves converge together and merge in from the sides to create a more powerful a-frame type of wave. a wedge can be created by a reflected wave bouncing off an obstacle like a jetty, rock, or wall and then merging with the original part of the wave that came straight in. a wedge can also be created by a portion of the wave refracting or wrapping in from deeper water like a channel or underwater canyon to merge with the original part of the wave coming straight in. wedges create good shaped waves with rights and lefts, along with more powerful waves than normal, which naturally attract good surfers.

weeps. something that is really lame or just all around bad; "Yo brah! That stinbomb you dropped was the weeps."

wettie warmer. the act of urinating in one's wetsuit.

white caps. ocean chop created by winds greater than 12 knots. as the wind increases the chop height also increases to a point where the chop becomes so steep and unstable the crest crumbles and breaks creating white water; choppy conditions with white caps are bad for surfing.

wicked. a one-word description of something that was really good; a good go-out would be deemed as wicked fun.

width. a term used to describe the surfboard dimension from rail-to-rail, measured at several key points by the shaper or manufacturer.

wind chop. waves produced by winds blowing onshore near a surf spot; characterized by white caps and generally choppy or churning seas; not good for surfing.

wind swell. waves produced by local vicinity surface winds; characterized by generally unorganized conditions; shifty peaks, whitecaps, chop; generally not good for surfing.

wind duration. in wave forecasting, the length of time the wind blows in the same direction over the swell generating area, or the fetch; one of the three key elements in the fundamental wave generation formula, along with wind velocity and fetch length, used to determine wave heights and wave periods in a storm- or wave-generating area.

wind surge. the increase in mean sea level caused by the "piling up" of water on the coastline by wind.

wind swell. a type of swell with a swell period of less than 11 seconds between successive waves. as a rule, the harder the wind blows, and the longer it blows over a longer distance of ocean, the bigger the swell will be and the longer the swell period will be between successive waves. the longer the swell period, the deeper the swell energy extends below the ocean surface, which interacts more with the ocean floor, or the "ground" so to speak; wind swells are typically "shallow water" swells because they are always generated by local winds with brief duration and over a limited distance of ocean. wind swell energy doesn't extend very deep below the ocean surface due to the shorter swell period. as such wind swells wrap (refract) very little into spots compared to ground swells which have longer swell periods and can wrap greatly into spots.

wind velocity. in wave forecasting, the speed of the wind as it blows in the same direction over the swell generating area, or the fetch. wind velocity is one of the three key elements in the fundamental wave generation formula, along with wind duration and fetch length, used to determine wave heights and wave periods in a storm- or wave-generating area.

wind waves. the combination of short period waves initially developed by the wind blowing over the ocean surface; the combination of these wind waves is called sea state, which is the mix of wave heights, periods and wavelengths.

winds on it. description of conditions when there is too much wind blowing which causes the swell to be chopped and sectioned.

windward. of or on the side of an island or point break exposed to the wind or to prevailing winds.

wing. a cutaway in the tail outline credited to Terry Fitzgerald of oz in 1971, designed to break the rail line in turns at high speeds; later reborn as the "Clayton Wing", a bump in the outline area around the front fins.

wipe out. a fall; a spectacular fall.

woody. originally coined as a name of the predecessor automobile that resembled a modern day station wagon. proved practical for surfers because of its construction; aptly named as many of its various panels were made of wood.

worked. the action a wave plays on you; similar to being under water in a hot tub.

Y

yak. to expel substance from one's mouth; generally caused from ingesting too much salt water after being rag dolled, held down or just plain worked; barf, drive-the-bus, beads, etc.

yo. exclamation used by a surfer to gain the attention of another person.

you should have been here yesterday. a phrase used to describe previous conditions of the day before; mostly used when a surfer wants to rant about his/her go out to someone who missed it.

Z

zimzala. free-spirited person who finds peace with the sand between toes.

zipload. to have or experience something to excess.

zoo, zooed. term used to describe a crowded surf lineup; as in "Dude, the lineup is a zoo today."

zulu. same as GMT or Greenwich Mean Time; zulu time is used on weather charts which may display 12z for 1200 gmt, or 00z for 0000 GMT; see GMT.

Additional Reading

For more of the terms contained in this book as well as newest surf lingo terms, descriptions and definitions, see the *Riptionary.com—Surf Lingo Lexicon*. The website can be found at http://www.riptionary.com or by pointing your browser to riptionary.com.

If you're just beginning to surf or are interested in starting, a good resource to consult is *Learn to Surf* by James MacClaren. The Lyons Press; (May 1, 1997), ISBN: 1558215689. *Learn to Surf* is an introductory guide to the sport that teaches the fundamentals of surfing with detailed, step-by-step instructions for the beginner.

For a historical perspective on the sport of surfing there is a comprehensive, website called *"From Polynesia with Love. The History of Surfing From Captain Cook to the Present."* by Ben Marcus. The website's history section can be found at http://www.surfingforlife.com/history.html.

If you want the daddy of all reference works for the sport of surfing, *The Encyclopedia of Surfing* by Matt Warshaw, Harcourt; 1st edition (October 6, 2003), ISBN: 151005796 is the most comprehensive review of the people, places, events, equipment, vernacular, and history of surfing ever compiled. It's a huge collection of expert knowledge, stories, and little-known trivia surrounding the sport.

0-595-31100-8

CPSIA information can be obtained at www.ICGtesting.com
Printed in the USA
LVOW10s1225110115

422375LV00002BA/289/P